The Comedy Of Errors (Large Print)

By

William Shakespeare

The Echo Library 2006

Published by

The Echo Library

Echo Library
131 High St.
Teddington
MiddlesexTW11 8HH

www.echolibrary.com

Please report serious faults in the text to
complaints@echolibrary.com

ISBN 1-84702-748-2

DRAMATIS PERSONAE

Solinus, Duke of Ephesus
Aegeon, a merchant of Syracuse

Antipholus Of Ephesus) twin brothers and
Antipholus Of Syracuse) sons to Aegion and
Aemelia

Dromio Of Ephesus) twin brothers, and
Dromio Of Syracuse   ) attendants on the
two Antipholuses

Balthazar, a merchant
Angelo, a goldsmith
First Merchant, friend to Antipholus of
Syracuse
Second Merchant, to whom Angelo is a
debtor
Pinch,a schoolmaster

Aemilia, wife to AEgeon; an abbess at
Ephesus
Adriana, wife to Antipholus of Ephesus
Luciana, her sister
Luce, servant to Adriana

A Courtezan

Gaoler, Officers, Attendants

SCENE:
Ephesus

ACT I. SCENE 1

A hall in the DUKE'S palace
*Enter the DUKE OF EPHESUS, AEGEON, the
Merchant of Syracuse, GAOLER, OFFICERS, and
other ATTENDANTS*

AEGEON.
Proceed, Solinus, to procure my fall, And by
the doom of death end woes and all.
DUKE.
Merchant of Syracuse, plead no more;
I am not partial to infringe our laws.
The enmity and discord which of late
Sprung from the rancorous outrage of your
duke
To merchants, our welldealing countrymen,
Who, wanting guilders to redeem their lives,
Have seal'd his rigorous statutes with their
bloods,
Excludes all pity from our threat'ning looks.
For, since the mortal and intestine jars
'Twixt thy seditious countrymen and us,
It hath in solemn synods been decreed,
Both by the Syracusians and ourselves,
To admit no traffic to our adverse towns;
Nay, more: if any born at Ephesus

Be seen at any Syracusian marts and fairs;
Again, if any Syracusian born
Come to the bay of Ephesushe dies,
His goods confiscate to the Duke's dispose,
Unless a thousand marks be levied,
To quit the penalty and to ransom him.
Thy substance, valued at the highest rate,
Cannot amount unto a hundred marks;
Therefore by law thou art condemn'd to die.
AEGEON.
Yet this my comfort: when your words are done,
My woes end likewise with the evening sun.
DUKE.
Well, Syracusian, say in brief the cause
Why thou departed'st from thy native home,
And for what cause thou cam'st to Ephesus.
AEGEON.
A heavier task could not have been impos'd
Than I to speak my griefs unspeakable;
Yet, that the world may witness that my end
Was wrought by nature, not by vile offence,
I'll utter what my sorrow gives me leave.
In Syracuse was I born, and wed
Unto a woman, happy but for me,

And by me, had not our hap been bad.
With her I liv'd in joy; our wealth increas'd
By prosperous voyages I often made
To Epidamnum; till my factor's death,
And the great care of goods at random left,
Drew me from kind embracements of my
spouse:
From whom my absence was not six months
old,
Before herself, almost at fainting under
The pleasing punishment that women bear,
Had made provision for her following me,
And soon and safe arrived where I was.
There had she not been long but she
became
A joyful mother of two goodly sons;
And, which was strange, the one so like the
other
As could not be disdnguish'd but by names.
That very hour, and in the selfsame inn,
A mean woman was delivered
Of such a burden, male twins, both alike.
Those, for their parents were exceeding
poor,
I bought, and brought up to attend my sons.
My wife, not meanly proud of two such

boys,
Made daily motions for our home return;
Unwilling, I agreed. Alas! too soon
We came aboard.
A league from Epidamnum had we sail'd
Before the alwayswindobeying deep
Gave any tragic instance of our harm:
But longer did we not retain much hope,
For what obscured light the heavens did
grant
Did but convey unto our fearful minds
A doubtful warrant of immediate death;
Which though myself would gladly have
embrac'd,
Yet the incessant weepings of my wife,
Weeping before for what she saw must
come,
And piteous plainings of the pretty babes,
That mourn'd for fashion, ignorant what to
fear,
Forc'd me to seek delays for them and me.
And this it was, for other means was none:
The sailors sought for safety by our boat,
And left the ship, then sinkingripe, to us;
My wife, more careful for the latterborn,
Had fast'ned him unto a small spare mast,

Such as seafaring men provide for storms;
To him one of the other twins was bound,
Whilst I had been like heedful of the other.
The children thus dispos'd, my wife and I,
Fixing our eyes on whom our care was fix'd,
Fast'ned ourselves at either end the mast,
And, floating straight, obedient to the stream,
Was carried towards Corinth, as we thought.
At length the sun, gazing upon the earth,
Dispers'd those vapours that offended us;
And, by the benefit of his wished light,
The seas wax'd calm, and we discovered
Two ships from far making amain to us
Of Corinth that, of Epidaurus this.
But ere they cameO, let me say no more!
Gather the sequel by that went before.

DUKE.

Nay, forward, old man, do not break off so;
For we may pity, though not pardon thee.

AEGEON.

O, had the gods done so, I had not now
Worthily term'd them merciless to us!
For, ere the ships could meet by twice five leagues,
We were encount'red by a mighty rock,

Which being violently borne upon,
Our helpful ship was splitted in the midst;
So that, in this unjust divorce of us,
Fortune had left to both of us alike
What to delight in, what to sorrow for.
Her part, poor soul, seeming as burdened
With lesser weight, but not with lesser woe,
Was carried with more speed before the
wind;
And in our sight they three were taken up
By fishermen of Corinth, as we thought.
At length another ship had seiz'd on us;
And, knowing whom it was their hap to
save,
Gave healthful welcome to their shipwreck'd
guests,
And would have reft the fishers of their
prey,
Had not their bark been very slow of sail;
And therefore homeward did they bend their
course.
Thus have you heard me sever'd from my
bliss,
That by misfortunes was my life prolong'd,
To tell sad stories of my own mishaps.
DUKE.

And, for the sake of them thou sorrowest for,
Do me the favour to dilate at full
What have befall'n of them and thee till now.

AEGEON.
My youngest boy, and yet my eldest care,
At eighteen years became inquisitive
After his brother, and importun'd me
That his attendantso his case was like,
Reft of his brother, but retain'd his name
Might bear him company in the quest of him;
Whom whilst I laboured of a love to see,
I hazarded the loss of whom I lov'd.
Five summers have I spent in farthest Greece,
Roaming clean through the bounds of Asia,
And, coasting homeward, came to Ephesus;
Hopeless to find, yet loath to leave unsought
Or that or any place that harbours men.
But here must end the story of my life;
And happy were I in my timely death,
Could all my travels warrant me they live.

DUKE.
Hapless, Aegeon, whom the fates have mark'd
To bear the extremity of dire mishap!
Now, trust me, were it not against our laws,
Against my crown, my oath, my dignity,
Which princes, would they, may not disannul,
My soul should sue as advocate for thee.
But though thou art adjudged to the death,
And passed sentence may not be recall'd
But to our honour's great disparagement,
Yet will I favour thee in what I can.
Therefore, merchant, I'll limit thee this day
To seek thy help by beneficial hap.
Try all the friends thou hast in Ephesus;
Beg thou, or borrow, to make up the sum,
And live; if no, then thou art doom'd to die.
Gaoler, take him to thy custody.
GAOLER.
I will, my lord.
AEGEON.
Hopeless and helpless doth Aegeon wend,
But to procrastinate his lifeless end.
Exeunt

SCENE 2

The mart
Enter Antipholus Of Syracuse, Dromio Of Syracuse, and First Merchant

FIRST MERCHANT.
Therefore, give out you are of Epidamnum,
Lest that your goods too soon be confiscate.
This very day a Syracusian merchant
Is apprehended for arrival here;
And, not being able to buy out his life,
According to the statute of the town,
Dies ere the weary sun set in the west.
There is your money that I had to keep.

ANTIPHOLUS OF SYRACUSE.
Go bear it to the Centaur, where we host.
And stay there, Dromio, till I come to thee.
Within this hour it will be dinnertime;
Till that, I'll view the manners of the town,
Peruse the traders, gaze upon the buildings,
And then return and sleep within mine inn;
For with long travel I am stiff and weary.
Get thee away.

DROMIO OF SYRACUSE.
Many a man would take you at your word,
And go indeed, having so good a mean.

Exit
ANTIPHOLUS OF SYRACUSE.
A trusty villain, sir, that very oft,
When I am dull with care and melancholy,
Lightens my humour with his merry jests.
What, will you walk with me about the town,
And then go to my inn and dine with me?
FIRST MERCHANT.
I am invited, sir, to certain merchants,
Of whom I hope to make much benefit;
I crave your pardon. Soon at five o'clock,
Please you, I'll meet with you upon the mart,
And afterward consort you till bed time.
My present business calls me from you now.
ANTIPHOLUS OF SYRACUSE.
Farewell till then. I will go lose myself,
And wander up and down to view the city.
FIRST MERCHANT.
Sir, I commend you to your own content.
Exit FIRST MERCHANT
ANTIPHOLUS OF SYRACUSE.
 He that commends me to mine own content
Commends me to the thing I cannot get.
I to the world am like a drop of water

That in the ocean seeks another drop,
Who, falling there to find his fellow forth,
Unseen, inquisitive, confounds himself.
So I, to find a mother and a brother,
In quest of them, unhappy, lose myself.

Enter Dromio Of Ephesus

Here comes the almanac of my true date.
What now? How chance thou art return'd so soon?

DROMIO OF EPHESUS.

Return'd so soon! rather approach'd too late.
The capon burns, the pig falls from the spit;
The clock hath strucken twelve upon the bell
My mistress made it one upon my cheek;
She is so hot because the meat is cold,
The meat is cold because you come not home,
You come not home because you have no stomach,
You have no stomach, having broke your fast;
But we, that know what 'tis to fast and pray,
Are penitent for your default today.
Antipholus Of Syracuse.

Stop in your wind, sir; tell me this, I pray:
Where have you left the money that I gave
you?

DROMIO OF EPHESUS.

OSixpence that I had a Wednesday last
To pay the saddler for my mistress'
crupper?
The saddler had it, sir; I kept it not.

ANTIPHOLUS OF SYRACUSE.

 I am not in a sportive humour now;
Tell me, and dally not, where is the money?
We being strangers here, how dar'st thou
trust
So great a charge from thine own custody?

DROMIO OF EPHESUS.

I pray you jest, sir, as you sit at dinner.
I from my mistress come to you in post;
If I return, I shall be post indeed,
For she will score your fault upon my pate.
Methinks your maw, like mine, should be
your clock,
And strike you home without a messenger.

ANTIPHOLUS OF SYRACUSE.

Come, Dromio, come, these jests are out of
season;
Reserve them till a merrier hour than this.

Where is the gold I gave in charge to thee?
DROMIO OF EPHESUS.
To me, sir? Why, you gave no gold to me.
ANTIPHOLUS OF SYRACUSE.
Come on, sir knave, have done your foolishness,
And tell me how thou hast dispos'd thy charge.
DROMIO OF EPHESUS.
My charge was but to fetch you from the mart
Home to your house, the Phoenix, sir, to dinner.
My mistress and her sister stays for you.
ANTIPHOLUS OF SYRACUSE.
Now, as I am a Christian, answer me
In what safe place you have bestow'd my money,
Or I shall break that merry sconce of yours,
That stands on tricks when I am undispos'd.
Where is the thousand marks thou hadst of me?
DROMIO OF EPHESUS.
I have some marks of yours upon my pate,
Some of my mistress' marks upon my shoulders,

But not a thousand marks between you
both.
If I should pay your worship those again,
Perchance you will not bear them patiently.

ANTIPHOLUS OF SYRACUSE.
Thy mistress' marks! What mistress, slave,
hast thou?

DROMIO OF EPHESUS.
Your worship's wife, my mistress at the
Phoenix;
She that doth fast till you come home to
dinner,
And prays that you will hie you home to
dinner.

ANTIPHOLUS OF SYRACUSE.
What, wilt thou flout me thus unto my face,
Being forbid? There, take you that, sir
knave.

[Beats him]

DROMIO OF EPHESUS.
What mean you, sir? For God's sake hold
your hands!
Nay, an you will not, sir, I'll take my heels.

Exit

ANTIPHOLUS OF SYRACUSE.
Upon my life, by some device or other

The villain is o'erraught of all my money.
They say this town is full of cozenage;
As, nimble jugglers that deceive the eye,
Darkworking sorcerers that change the
mind,
Soulkilling witches that deform the body,
Disguised cheaters, prating mountebanks,
And many suchlike liberties of sin;
If it prove so, I will be gone the sooner.
I'll to the Centaur to go seek this slave.
I greatly fear my money is not safe.
Exit

ACT II. SCENE 1

The house of Antipholus Of Ephesus
Enter Adriana, wife to Antipholus Of
Ephesus, with Luciana, her sister
ADRIANA.
Neither my husband nor the slave return'd
That in such haste I sent to seek his master!
Sure, Luciana, it is two o'clock.
LUCIANA.
Perhaps some merchant hath invited him,
And from the mart he's somewhere gone to
dinner;
Good sister, let us dine, and never fret.
A man is master of his liberty;
Time is their master, and when they see
time,
They'll go or come. If so, be patient, sister.
ADRIANA.
Why should their liberty than ours be more?
LUCIANA.
Because their business still lies out o' door.
ADRIANA.
Look when I serve him so, he takes it ill.
LUCIANA.
O, know he is the bridle of your will.

ADRIANA.
There's none but asses will be bridled so.
LUCIANA.
Why, headstrong liberty is lash'd with woe.
There's nothing situate under heaven's eye
But hath his bound, in earth, in sea, in sky.
The beasts, the fishes, and the winged fowls,
Are their males' subjects, and at their controls.
Man, more divine, the master of all these,
Lord of the wide world and wild wat'ry seas,
Indu'd with intellectual sense and souls,
Of more preeminence than fish and fowls,
Are masters to their females, and their lords;
Then let your will attend on their accords.
ADRIANA.
This servitude makes you to keep unwed.
LUCIANA.
Not this, but troubles of the marriagebed.
ADRIANA.
But, were you wedded, you would bear some sway.
LUCIANA.
Ere I learn love, I'll practise to obey.

ADRIANA.

How if your husband start some other where?

LUCIANA.

Till he come home again, I would forbear.

ADRIANA.

Patience unmov'd! no marvel though she pause:

They can be meek that have no other cause.

A wretched soul, bruis'd with adversity,

We bid be quiet when we hear it cry;

But were we burd'ned with like weight of pain,

As much, or more, we should ourselves complain.

So thou, that hast no unkind mate to grieve thee,

With urging helpless patience would relieve me;

But if thou live to see like right bereft,

This foolbegg'd patience in thee will be left.

LUCIANA.

Well, I will marry one day, but to try.

Here comes your man, now is your husband nigh.

Enter Dromio Of Ephesus

ADRIANA.
Say, is your tardy master now at hand?
DROMIO OF EPHESUS.
Nay, he's at two hands with me, and that
my two ears can witness.
ADRIANA.
Say, didst thou speak with him? Know'st
thou his mind?
DROMIO OF EPHESUS.
Ay, ay, he told his mind upon mine ear.
Beshrew his hand, I scarce could understand
it.
LUCIANA.
Spake he so doubtfully thou could'st not
feel his meaning?
DROMIO OF EPHESUS.
Nay, he struck so plainly I could to well feel
his blows; and withal so doubtfully that I
could scarce understand them.
ADRIANA.
But say, I prithee, is he coming home?
It seems he hath great care to please his
wife.
DROMIO OF EPHESUS.
Why, mistress, sure my master is hornmad.
ADRIANA.

Hornmad, thou villain!
DROMIO OF EPHESUS.
I mean not cuckoldmad;
But, sure, he is stark mad.
When I desir'd him to come home to dinner,
He ask'd me for a thousand marks in gold.
"Tis dinner time' quoth I; 'My gold!' quoth
he.
'Your meat doth burn' quoth I; 'My gold!'
quoth he.
'Will you come home?' quoth I; 'My gold!'
quoth he.
'Where is the thousand marks I gave thee,
villain?'
'The pig' quoth I 'is burn'd'; 'My gold!' quoth
he.
'My mistress, sir,' quoth I; 'Hang up thy
mistress;
I know not thy mistress; out on thy
mistress.'
LUCIANA.
Quoth who?
DROMIO OF EPHESUS.
Quoth my master.
'I know' quoth he 'no house, no wife, no
mistress.'

So that my errand, due unto my tongue,
I thank him, I bare home upon my
shoulders;
For, in conclusion, he did beat me there.
ADRIANA.
Go back again, thou slave, and fetch him
home.
DROMIO OF EPHESUS.
Go back again, and be new beaten home?
For God's sake, send some other messenger.
ADRIANA.
Back, slave, or I will break thy pate across.
DROMIO OF EPHESUS.
And he will bless that cross with other
beating;
Between you I shall have a holy head.
ADRIANA.
Hence, prating peasant! Fetch thy master
home.
DROMIO OF EPHESUS.
Am I so round with you, as you with me,
That like a football you do spurn me thus?
You spurn me hence, and he will spurn me
hither;
If I last in this service, you must case me in
leather.

Exit

LUCIANA.

Fie, how impatience loureth in your face!

ADRIANA.

His company must do his minions grace,
Whilst I at home starve for a merry look.
Hath homely age th' alluring beauty took
From my poor cheek? Then he hath wasted
it.
Are my discourses dull? Barren my wit?
If voluble and sharp discourse be marr'd,
Unkindness blunts it more than marble
hard.
Do their gay vestments his affections bait?
That's not my fault; he's master of my
state.
What ruins are in me that can be found
By him not ruin'd? Then is he the ground
Of my defeatures. My decayed fair
A sunny look of his would soon repair.
But, too unruly deer, he breaks the pale,
And feeds from home; poor I am but his
stale.

LUCIANA.

Selfharming jealousy! fie, beat it hence.

ADRIANA.

Unfeeling fools can with such wrongs
dispense.
I know his eye doth homage otherwhere;
Or else what lets it but he would be here?
Sister, you know he promis'd me a chain;
Would that alone a love he would detain,
So he would keep fair quarter with his bed!
I see the jewel best enamelled
Will lose his beauty; yet the gold bides still
That others touch and, often touching, will
Where gold; and no man that hath a name
By falsehood and corruption doth it shame.
Since that my beauty cannot please his eye,
I'll weep what's left away, and weeping die.
Luciana.
How many fond fools serve mad jealousy!
Exeunt

SCENE 2

The mart
Enter Antipholus Of Syracuse
ANTIPHOLUS OF SYRACUSE.
The gold I gave to Dromio is laid up
Safe at the Centaur, and the heedful slave
Is wand'red forth in care to seek me out.
By computation and mine host's report
I could not speak with Dromio since at first
I sent him from the mart. See, here he comes.
Enter Dromio Of Syracuse
How now, sir, is your merry humour alter'd?
As you love strokes, so jest with me again.
You know no Centaur! You receiv'd no gold!
Your mistress sent to have me home to dinner!
My house was at the Phoenix! Wast thou mad,
That thus so madly thou didst answer me?
DROMIO OF SYRACUSE.
What answer, sir? When spake I such a word?
ANTIPHOLUS OF SYRACUSE.
Even now, even here, not half an hour since.

28

DROMIO OF SYRACUSE.
I did not see you since you sent me hence,
Home to the Centaur, with the gold you
gave me.
ANTIPHOLUS OF SYRACUSE.
Villain, thou didst deny the gold's receipt,
And told'st me of a mistress and a dinner;
For which, I hope, thou felt'st I was
displeas'd.
DROMIO OF SYRACUSE.
I am glad to see you in this merry vein.
What means this jest? I pray you, master,
tell me.
ANTIPHOLUS OF SYRACUSE.
Yea, dost thou jeer and flout me in the
teeth?
Think'st thou I jest? Hold, take thou that,
and that.
[Beating him]
DROMIO OF SYRACUSE.
Hold, sir, for God's sake! Now your jest is
earnest.
Upon what bargain do you give it me?
ANTIPHOLUS OF SYRACUSE.
Because that I familiarly sometimes
Do use you for my fool and chat with you,

Your sauciness will jest upon my love,
And make a common of my serious hours.
When the sun shines let foolish gnats make
sport,
But creep in crannies when he hides his
beams.
If you will jest with me, know my aspect,
And fashion your demeanour to my looks,
Or I will beat this method in your sconce.
DROMIO OF SYRACUSE.
Sconce, call you it? So you would leave
battering, I had rather have it a head. An
you use these blows long, I must get a
sconce for my head, and insconce it too; or
else I shall seek my wit in my shoulders.
But I pray, sir, why am I beaten?
ANTIPHOLUS OF SYRACUSE.
Dost thou not know?
DROMIO OF SYRACUSE.
Nothing, sir, but that I am beaten.
ANTIPHOLUS OF SYRACUSE.
Shall I tell you why?
DROMIO OF SYRACUSE.
Ay, sir, and wherefore; for they say every
why hath a wherefore.

ANTIPHOLUS OF SYRACUSE.
Why, first for flouting me; and then wherefore,
For urging it the second time to me.
DROMIO OF SYRACUSE.
Was there ever any man thus beaten out of season,
When in the why and the wherefore is neither rhyme nor reason?
Well, sir, I thank you.
ANTIPHOLUS OF SYRACUSE.
Thank me, sir! for what?
DROMIO OF SYRACUSE.
Marry, sir, for this something that you gave me for nothing.
ANTIPHOLUS OF SYRACUSE.
I'll make you amends next, to give you nothing for something. But say, sir, is it dinnertime?
DROMIO OF SYRACUSE.
No, sir; I think the meat wants that I have.
ANTIPHOLUS OF SYRACUSE.
In good time, sir, what's that?
DROMIO OF SYRACUSE.
Basting.

ANTIPHOLUS OF SYRACUSE.
Well, sir, then 'twill be dry.
DROMIO OF SYRACUSE.
If it be, sir, I pray you eat none of it.
ANTIPHOLUS OF SYRACUSE.
Your reason?
DROMIO OF SYRACUSE.
Lest it make you choleric, and purchase me
another dry basting.
ANTIPHOLUS OF SYRACUSE.
Well, sir, learn to jest in good time; there's
a time for all things.
DROMIO OF SYRACUSE.
I durst have denied that, before you were so
choleric.
ANTIPHOLUS OF SYRACUSE.
By what rule, sir?
DROMIO OF SYRACUSE.
Marry, sir, by a rule as plain as the plain
bald pate of Father Time himself.
ANTIPHOLUS OF SYRACUSE.
Let's hear it.
DROMIO OF SYRACUSE.
There's no time for a man to recover his hair
that grows bald by nature.

ANTIPHOLUS OF SYRACUSE.
May he not do it by fine and recovery?
DROMIO OF SYRACUSE.
Yes, to pay a fine for a periwig, and recover the lost hair of another man.
ANTIPHOLUS OF SYRACUSE.
Why is Time such a niggard ofhair, being, as it is, so plentiful an excrement?
DROMIO OF SYRACUSE.
Because it is a blessing that he bestows on beasts, and what he hath scanted men in hair he hath given them in wit.
ANTIPHOLUS OF SYRACUSE.
Why, but there's many a man hath more hair than wit.
DROMIO OF SYRACUSE.
Not a man of those but he hath the wit to lose his hair.
ANTIPHOLUS OF SYRACUSE.
Why, thou didst conclude hairy men plain dealers without wit.
DROMIO OF SYRACUSE.
The plainer dealer, the sooner lost; yet he loseth it in a kind of jollity.
ANTIPHOLUS OF SYRACUSE.
For what reason?

DROMIO OF SYRACUSE.
For two; and sound ones too.
ANTIPHOLUS OF SYRACUSE.
Nay, not sound I pray you.
DROMIO OF SYRACUSE.
Sure ones, then.
ANTIPHOLUS OF SYRACUSE.
Nay, not sure, in a thing falsing.
DROMIO OF SYRACUSE.
Certain ones, then.
ANTIPHOLUS OF SYRACUSE.
Name them.
DROMIO OF SYRACUSE.
The one, to save the money that he spends in tiring; the other, that at dinner they should not drop in his porridge.
ANTIPHOLUS OF SYRACUSE.
You would all this time have prov'd there is no time for all things.
DROMIO OF SYRACUSE.
Marry, and did, sir; namely, no time to recover hair lost by nature.
ANTIPHOLUS OF SYRACUSE.
But your reason was not substantial, why there is no time to recover.

DROMIO OF SYRACUSE.
Thus I mend it: Time himself is bald, and
therefore to the world's end will have bald
followers.
ANTIPHOLUS OF SYRACUSE.
I knew 't'would be a bald conclusion. But,
soft, who wafts us yonder?
Enter Adriana and Luciana
ADRIANA.
Ay, ay, Antipholus, look strange and frown.
Some other mistress hath thy sweet
aspects;
I am not Adriana, nor thy wife.
The time was once when thou unurg'd
wouldst vow
That never words were music to thine ear,
That never object pleasing in thine eye,
That never touch well welcome to thy hand,
That never meat sweetsavour'd in thy taste,
Unless I spake, or look'd, or touch'd, or
carv'd to thee.
How comes it now, my husband, O, how
comes it,
That thou art then estranged from thyself?
Thyself I call it, being strange to me,
That, undividable, incorporate,

Am better than thy dear self's better part.
Ah, do not tear away thyself from me;
For know, my love, as easy mayst thou fall
A drop of water in the breaking gulf,
And take unmingled thence that drop again
Without addition or diminishing,
As take from me thyself, and not me too.
How dearly would it touch thee to the quick,
Should'st thou but hear I were licentious,
And that this body, consecrate to thee,
By ruffian lust should be contaminate!
Wouldst thou not spit at me and spurn at
me,
And hurl the name of husband in my face,
And tear the stain'd skin off my harlotbrow,
And from my false hand cut the
weddingring,
And break it with a deepdivorcing vow?
I know thou canst, and therefore see thou
do it.
I am possess'd with an adulterate blot;
My blood is mingled with the crime of lust;
For if we two be one, and thou play false,
I do digest the poison of thy flesh,
Being strumpeted by thy contagion.
Keep then fair league and truce with thy

true bed;
I live disstain'd, thou undishonoured.
ANTIPHOLUS OF SYRACUSE.
Plead you to me, fair dame? I know you not:
In Ephesus I am but two hours old,
As strange unto your town as to your talk,
Who, every word by all my wit being
scann'd,
Wants wit in all one word to understand.
LUCIANA.
Fie, brother, how the world is chang'd with
you!
When were you wont to use my sister thus?
She sent for you by Dromio home to dinner.
ANTIPHOLUS OF SYRACUSE.
By Dromio?
DROMIO OF SYRACUSE.
By me?
ADRIANA.
By thee; and this thou didst return from him
That he did buffet thee, and in his blows
Denied my house for his, me for his wife.
ANTIPHOLUS OF SYRACUSE.
Did you converse, sir, with this
gentlewoman?
What is the course and drift of your

compact?

DROMIO OF SYRACUSE.
I, Sir? I never saw her till this time.

ANTIPHOLUS OF SYRACUSE.
Villain, thou liest; for even her very words
Didst thou deliver to me on the mart.

DROMIO OF SYRACUSE.
I never spake with her in all my life.

ANTIPHOLUS OF SYRACUSE.
How can she thus, then, call us by our names,
Unless it be by inspiration?

ADRIANA.
How ill agrees it with your gravity
To counterfeit thus grossly with your slave,
Abetting him to thwart me in my mood!
Be it my wrong you are from me exempt,
But wrong not that wrong with a more contempt.
Come, I will fasten on this sleeve of thine;
Thou art an elm, my husband, I a vine,
Whose weakness, married to thy stronger state,
Makes me with thy strength to communicate.
If aught possess thee from me, it is dross,

Usurping ivy, brier, or idle moss;
Who all, for want of pruning, with intrusion
Infect thy sap, and live on thy confusion.

ANTIPHOLUS OF SYRACUSE.

To me she speaks; she moves me for her
theme.
What, was I married to her in my dream?
Or sleep I now, and think I hear all this?
What error drives our eyes and ears amiss?
Until I know this sure uncertainty,
I'll entertain the offer'd fallacy.

LUCIANA.

Dromio, go bid the servants spread for
dinner.

DROMIO OF SYRACUSE.

O, for my beads! I cross me for sinner.
This is the fairy land. O spite of spites!
We talk with goblins, owls, and sprites.
If we obey them not, this will ensue:
They'll suck our breath, or pinch us black
and blue.

LUCIANA.

Why prat'st thou to thyself, and answer'st
not?
Dromio, thou drone, thou snail, thou slug,
thou sot!

DROMIO OF SYRACUSE.
I am transformed, master, am not I?
ANTIPHOLUS OF SYRACUSE.
I think thou art in mind, and so am I.
DROMIO OF SYRACUSE.
Nay, master, both in mind and in my shape.
ANTIPHOLUS OF SYRACUSE.
Thou hast thine own form.
DROMIO OF SYRACUSE.
No, I am an ape.
LUCIANA.
If thou art chang'd to aught, 'tis to an ass.
DROMIO OF SYRACUSE.
'Tis true; she rides me, and I long for grass.
'Tis so, I am an ass; else it could never be
But I should know her as well as she knows
me.
ADRIANA.
Come, come, no longer will I be a fool,
To put the finger in the eye and weep,
Whilst man and master laughs my woes to
scorn.
Come, sir, to dinner. Dromio, keep the gate.
Husband, I'll dine above with you today,
And shrive you of a thousand idle pranks.
Sirrah, if any ask you for your master,

Say he dines forth, and let no creature enter.
Come, sister. Dromio, play the porter well.
ANTIPHOLUS OF SYRACUSE.
Am I in earth, in heaven, or in hell?
Sleeping or waking, mad or well advis'd?
Known unto these, and to myself disguis'd!
I'll say as they say, and persever so,
And in this mist at all adventures go.
DROMIO OF SYRACUSE.
Master, shall I be porter at the gate?
ADRIANA.
Ay; and let none enter, lest I break your pate.
LUCIANA.
Come, come, Antipholus, we dine too late.
Exeunt

ACT III. SCENE 1

Before the house of Antipholus Of Ephesus
*Enter Antipholus Of Ephesus, Dromio Of
Ephesus, Angelo, and Balthazar*
ANTIPHOLUS OF EPHESUS.
Good Signior Angelo, you must excuse us
all;
My wife is shrewish when I keep not hours.
Say that I linger'd with you at your shop
To see the making of her carcanet,
And that tomorrow you will bring it home.
But here's a villain that would face me down
He met me on the mart, and that I beat him,
And charg'd him with a thousand marks in
gold,
And that I did deny my wife and house.
Thou drunkard, thou, what didst thou mean
by this?
DROMIO OF EPHESUS.
Say what you will, sir, but I know what I
know.
That you beat me at the mart I have your
hand to show;
If the skin were parchment, and the blows
you gave were ink,

Your own handwriting would tell you what I think.

ANTIPHOLUS OF EPHESUS.

I think thou art an ass.

DROMIO OF EPHESUS.

Marry, so it doth appear
By the wrongs I suffer and the blows I bear.
I should kick, being kick'd; and being at that pass,
You would keep from my heels, and beware of an ass.

ANTIPHOLUS OF EPHESUS.

Y'are sad, Signior Balthazar; pray God our cheer
May answer my good will and your good welcome here.

BALTHAZAR.

I hold your dainties cheap, sir, and your welcome dear.

ANTIPHOLUS OF EPHESUS.

O, Signior Balthazar, either at flesh or fish,
A table full of welcome makes scarce one dainty dish.

BALTHAZAR.

Good meat, sir, is common; that every churl affords.

ANTIPHOLUS OF EPHESUS.
And welcome more common; for that's nothing but words.
BALTHAZAR.
Small cheer and great welcome makes a merry feast.
ANTIPHOLUS OF EPHESUS.
Ay, to a niggardly host and more sparing guest.
But though my cates be mean, take them in good part;
Better cheer may you have, but not with better heart.
But, soft, my door is lock'd; go bid them let us in.
DROMIO OF EPHESUS.
Maud, Bridget, Marian, Cicely, Gillian, Ginn!
DROMIO OF SYRACUSE.
[Within] Mome, malt horse, capon, coxcomb, idiot, patch!
Either get thee from the door, or sit down at the hatch.
Dost thou conjure for wenches, that thou call'st for such store,
When one is one too many? Go get thee from the door.

DROMIO OF EPHESUS.
What patch is made our porter?
My master stays in the street.
DROMIO OF SYRACUSE.
Within]Let him walk from whence he came,
lest he catch cold on's feet.
ANTIPHOLUS OF EPHESUS.
Who talks within there? Ho, open the door!
DROMIO OF SYRACUSE.
Within]Right, sir; I'll tell you when, an you'll
tell me wherefore.
ANTIPHOLUS OF EPHESUS.
Wherefore? For my dinner;
I have not din'd today.
DROMIO OF SYRACUSE.
Within]Nor today here you must not; come
again when you may.
ANTIPHOLUS OF EPHESUS.
What art thou that keep'st me out from the
house I owe?
DROMIO OF SYRACUSE.
Within]The porter for this time, sir, and my
name is Dromio.
DROMIO OF EPHESUS.
O Villain, thou hast stol'n both mine office
and my name!

The one ne'er got me credit, the other mickle blame.

If thou hadst been Dromio today in my place,

Thou wouldst have chang'd thy face for a name, or thy name for an ass.

Enter Luce, within

LUCE.

*[Within]*What a coil is there, Dromio? Who are those at the gate?

DROMIO OF EPHESUS.

Let my master in, Luce.

LUCE.[Within]Faith, no, he comes too late;

And so tell your master.

DROMIO OF EPHESUS.

O Lord, I must laugh!

Have at you with a proverb: Shall I set in my staff?

LUCE.

*[Within]*Have at you with another: that'swhen? can you tell?

DROMIO OF SYRACUSE.

*[Within]*If thy name be called Luce

Luce, thou hast answer'd him well.

ANTIPHOLUS OF EPHESUS.

Do you hear, you minion? You'll let us in, I

hope?

LUCE.

[Within] I thought to have ask'd you.

DROMIO OF SYRACUSE.

[Within] And you said no.

DROMIO OF EPHESUS.

SO, Come, help: well struck! there was blow for blow.

ANTIPHOLUS OF EPHESUS.

Thou baggage, let me in.

LUCE.

[Within] Can you tell for whose sake?

DROMIO OF EPHESUS.

Master, knock the door hard.

LUCE.

[Within] Let him knock till it ache.

ANTIPHOLUS OF EPHESUS.

You'll cry for this, minion, if beat the door down.

LUCE.

[Within] What needs all that, and a pair of stocks in the town?

Enter Adriana, within

ADRIANA.

[Within] Who is that at the door, that keeps all this noise?

DROMIO OF SYRACUSE.
[Within] By my troth, your town is troubled with unruly boys.
ANTIPHOLUS OF EPHESUS.
Are you there, wife? You might have come before.
ADRIANA.
[Within] Your wife, sir knave! Go get you from the door.
DROMIO OF EPHESUS.
If YOU went in pain, master, this 'knave' would go sore.
ANGELO.
Here is neither cheer, sir, nor welcome; we would fain have either.
BALTHAZAR.
In debating which was best, we shall part with neither.
DROMIO OF EPHESUS.
They stand at the door, master; bid them welcome hither.
ANTIPHOLUS OF EPHESUS.
There is something in the wind, that we cannot get in.
DROMIO OF EPHESUS.
You would say so, master, if your garments

were thin.
Your cake here is warm within; you stand here in the cold;
It would make a man mad as a buck to be so bought and sold.

ANTIPHOLUS OF EPHESUS.
Go fetch me something; I'll break ope the gate.

DROMIO OF SYRACUSE.
[Within] Break any breaking here, and I'll break your knave's pate.

DROMIO OF EPHESUS.
A man may break a word with you, sir; and words are but wind;
Ay, and break it in your face, so he break it not behind.

DROMIO OF SYRACUSE.
[Within] It seems thou want'st breaking; out upon thee, hind!

DROMIO OF EPHESUS.
Here's too much 'out upon thee!' pray thee let me in.

DROMIO OF SYRACUSE.
[Within] Ay, when fowls have no feathers and fish have no fin.

ANTIPHOLUS OF EPHESUS.
Well, I'll break in; go borrow me a crow.
DROMIO OF EPHESUS.
A crow without feather? Master, mean you
so?
For a fish without a fin, there's a fowl
without a feather;
If a crow help us in, sirrah, we'll pluck a
crow together.
ANTIPHOLUS OF EPHESUS.
Go get thee gone; fetch me an iron crow.
BALTHAZAR.
Have patience, sir; O, let it not be so!
Herein you war against your reputation,
And draw within the compass of suspect
Th' unviolated honour of your wife.
Once thisyour long experience of her
wisdom,
Her sober virtue, years, and modesty,
Plead on her part some cause to you
unknown;
And doubt not, sir, but she will well excuse
Why at this time the doors are made against
you.
Be rul'd by me: depart in patience,
And let us to the Tiger all to dinner;

And, about evening, come yourself alone
To know the reason of this strange
restraint.
If by strong hand you offer to break in
Now in the stirring passage of the day,
A vulgar comment will be made of it,
And that supposed by the common rout
Against your yet ungalled estimation
That may with foul intrusion enter in
And dwell upon your grave when you are
dead;
For slander lives upon succession,
For ever hous'd where it gets possession.
ANTIPHOLUS OF EPHESUS.
You have prevail'd. I will depart in quiet,
And in despite of mirth mean to be merry.
I know a wench of excellent discourse,
Pretty and witty; wild, and yet, too, gentle;
There will we dine. This woman that I mean,
My wifebut, I protest, without desert
Hath oftentimes upbraided me withal;
To her will we to dinner.[To ANGELO]Get
you home
And fetch the chain; by this I know 'tis
made.
Bring it, I pray you, to the Porpentine;

For there's the house. That chain will I
bestow
Be it for nothing but to spite my wife
Upon mine hostess there; good sir, make
haste.
Since mine own doors refuse to entertain
me,
I'll knock elsewhere, to see if they'll disdain
me.

ANGELO.

I'll meet you at that place some hour hence.

ANTIPHOLUS OF EPHESUS.

Do so; this jest shall cost me some expense.
Exeunt

SCENE 2

Before the house of Antipholus Of Ephesus
Enter Luciana with Antipholus Of Syracuse
LUCIANA.
And may it be that you have quite forgot
A husband's office? Shall, Antipholus,
Even in the spring of love, thy lovesprings rot?
Shall love, in building, grow so ruinous?
If you did wed my sister for her wealth,
Then for her wealth's sake use her with more kindness;
Or, if you like elsewhere, do it by stealth;
Muffle your false love with some show of blindness;
Let not my sister read it in your eye;
Be not thy tongue thy own shame's orator;
Look sweet, speak fair, become disloyalty;
Apparel vice like virtue's harbinger;
Bear a fair presence, though your heart be tainted;
Teach sin the carriage of a holy saint;
Be secretfalse. What need she be acquainted?
What simple thief brags of his own attaint?

'Tis double wrong to truant with your bed
And let her read it in thy looks at board;
Shame hath a bastard fame, well managed;
Ill deeds is doubled with an evil word.
Alas, poor women! make us but believe,
Being compact of credit, that you love us;
Though others have the arm, show us the
sleeve;
We in your motion turn, and you may move
us.
Then, gentle brother, get you in again;
Comfort my sister, cheer her, call her wife.
'Tis holy sport to be a little vain
When the sweet breath of flattery conquers
strife.
ANTIPHOLUS OF SYRACUSE.
Sweet mistresswhat your name is else, I
know not,
Nor by what wonder you do hit of mine
Less in your knowledge and your grace you
show not
Than our earth's wondermore than earth,
divine.
Teach me, dear creature, how to think and
speak;
Lay open to my earthygross conceit,

Smoth'red in errors, feeble, shallow, weak,
The folded meaning of your words' deceit.
Against my soul's pure truth why labour you
To make it wander in an unknown field?
Are you a god? Would you create me new?
Transform me, then, and to your pow'r I'll
yield.
But if that I am I, then well I know
Your weeping sister is no wife of mine,
Nor to her bed no homage do I owe;
Far more, far more, to you do I decline.
O, train me not, sweet mermaid, with thy
note,
To drown me in thy sister's flood of tears.
Sing, siren, for thyself, and I will dote;
Spread o'er the silver waves thy golden
hairs,
And as a bed I'll take them, and there he;
And in that glorious supposition think
He gains by death that hath such means to
die.
Let Love, being light, be drowned if she
sink.
LUCIANA.
What, are you mad, that you do reason so?

ANTIPHOLUS OF SYRACUSE.
Not mad, but mated; how, I do not know.
LUCIANA.
It is a fault that springeth from your eye.
ANTIPHOLUS OF SYRACUSE.
For gazing on your beams, fair sun, being
by.
LUCIANA.
Gaze where you should, and that will clear
your sight.
ANTIPHOLUS OF SYRACUSE.
As good to wink, sweet love, as look on
night.
LUCIANA.
Why call you me love? Call my sister so.
ANTIPHOLUS OF SYRACUSE.
Thy sister's sister.
LUCIANA.
That's my sister.
ANTIPHOLUS OF SYRACUSE.
No; It is thyself, mine own self's better part;
Mine eye's clear eye, my dear heart's dearer
heart,
My food, my fortune, and my sweet hope's
aim,
My sole earth's heaven, and my heaven's

claim.

LUCIANA.

All this my sister is, or else should be.

ANTIPHOLUS OF SYRACUSE.

Call thyself sister, sweet, for I am thee;
Thee will I love, and with thee lead my life;
Thou hast no husband yet, nor I no wife.
Give me thy hand.

LUCIANA.

O, soft, sir, hold you still;
I'll fetch my sister to get her good will.

Exit Luciana
Enter Dromio Of Syracuse.

ANTIPHOLUS OF SYRACUSE.

Why, how now, Dromio! Where run'st thou
so fast?

DROMIO OF SYRACUSE.

Do you know me, sir? Am I Dromio?
Am I your man? Am I myself?

ANTIPHOLUS OF SYRACUSE.

Thou art Dromio, thou art my man, thou art
thyself.

DROMIO OF SYRACUSE.

I am an ass, I am a woman's man, and
besides myself.

ANTIPHOLUS OF SYRACUSE.
What woman's man, and how besides
thyself?
DROMIO OF SYRACUSE.
Marry, sir, besides myself, I am due to a
womanone that claims me, one that haunts
me, one that will have me.
ANTIPHOLUS OF SYRACUSE.
What claim lays she to thee?
DROMIO OF SYRACUSE.
Marry, sir, such claim as you would lay to
your horse; and she would have me as a
beast: not that, I being a beast, she would
have me; but that she, being a very beastly
creature, lays claim to me.
ANTIPHOLUS OF SYRACUSE.
What is she?
DROMIO OF SYRACUSE.
A very reverent body; ay, such a one as a
man may not speak of without he say
'Sirreverence.' I have but lean luck in the
match, and yet is she a wondrous fat
marriage.
ANTIPHOLUS OF SYRACUSE.
How dost thou mean a fat marriage?

DROMIO OF SYRACUSE.
Marry, sir, she's the kitchenwench, and all grease; and I know not what use to put her to but to make a lamp of her and run from her by her own light. I warrant, her rags and the tallow in them will burn Poland winter. If she lives till doomsday, she'll burn week longer than the whole world.

ANTIPHOLUS OF SYRACUSE.
What complexion is she of?

DROMIO OF SYRACUSE.
Swart, like my shoe; but her face nothing like so clean kept; for why, she sweats, a man may go over shoes in the grime of it.

ANTIPHOLUS OF SYRACUSE.
That's a fault that water will mend.

DROMIO OF SYRACUSE.
No, sir, 'tis in grain; Noah's flood could not do it.

ANTIPHOLUS OF SYRACUSE.
What's her name?

DROMIO OF SYRACUSE.
Nell, sir; but her name and three quarters, that's an ell and three quarters, will not measure her from hip to hip.

ANTIPHOLUS OF SYRACUSE.
Then she bears some breadth?
DROMIO OF SYRACUSE.
No longer from head to foot than from hip
to hip: she is spherical, like a globe; I could
find out countries in her.
ANTIPHOLUS OF SYRACUSE.
In what part of her body stands Ireland?
DROMIO OF SYRACUSE.
Marry, sir, in her buttocks; I found it out by
the bogs.
ANTIPHOLUS OF SYRACUSE.
Where Scotland?
DROMIO OF SYRACUSE.
I found it by the barrenness, hard in the
palm of the hand.
ANTIPHOLUS OF SYRACUSE.
Where France?
DROMIO OF SYRACUSE.
In her forehead, arm'd and reverted, making
war against her heir.
ANTIPHOLUS OF SYRACUSE.
Where England?
DROMIO OF SYRACUSE.
I look'd for the chalky cliffs, but I could find
no whiteness in them; but I guess it stood in

her chin, by the salt rheum that ran
between France and it.

ANTIPHOLUS OF SYRACUSE.
Where Spain?

DROMIO OF SYRACUSE.
Faith, I saw it not, but I felt it hot in her
breath.

ANTIPHOLUS OF SYRACUSE.
Where America, the Indies?

DROMIO OF SYRACUSE.
O, sir, upon her nose, an o'er embellished
with rubies, carbuncles, sapphires, declining
their rich aspect to the hot breath of Spain;
who sent whole armadoes of caracks to be
ballast at her nose.

ANTIPHOLUS OF SYRACUSE.
Where stood Belgia, the Netherlands?

DROMIO OF SYRACUSE.
O, Sir, I did not look so low. To conclude:
this drudge or diviner laid claim to me;
call'd me
Dromio; swore I was assur'd to her; told me
what privy marks I had about me, as, the
mark of my shoulder, the mole in my neck,
the great wart on my left arm, that I,
amaz'd, ran from her as a witch.

And, I think, if my breast had not been
made of faith, and my heart of steel,
She had transform'd me to a curtal dog, and
made me turn i' th' wheel.

ANTIPHOLUS OF SYRACUSE.
Go hie thee presently post to the road;
An if the wind blow any way from shore,
I will not harbour in this town tonight.
If any bark put forth, come to the mart,
Where I will walk till thou return to me.
If every one knows us, and we know none,
'Tis time, I think, to trudge, pack and be
gone.

DROMIO OF SYRACUSE.
As from a bear a man would run for life,
So fly I from her that would be my wife.
Exit

ANTIPHOLUS OF SYRACUSE.
There's none but witches do inhabit here,
And therefore 'tis high time that I were
hence.
She that doth call me husband, even my
soul
Doth for a wife abhor. But her fair sister,
Possess'd with such a gentle sovereign
grace,

Of such enchanting presence and discourse,
Hath almost made me traitor to myself;
But, lest myself be guilty to selfwrong,
I'll stop mine ears against the mermaid's
song.

Enter Angelo with the chain

ANGELO.
Master Antipholus!

ANTIPHOLUS OF SYRACUSE.
Ay, that's my name.

ANGELO.
I know it well, sir. Lo, here is the chain.
I thought to have ta'en you at the
Porpentine;
The chain unfinish'd made me stay thus
long.

ANTIPHOLUS OF SYRACUSE.
What is your will that I shall do with this?

ANGELO.
What please yourself, sir; I have made it for
you.

ANTIPHOLUS OF SYRACUSE.
Made it for me, sir! I bespoke it not.

ANGELO.
Not once nor twice, but twenty times you
have.

Go home with it, and please your wife withal;
And soon at suppertime I'll visit you,
And then receive my money for the chain.
ANTIPHOLUS OF SYRACUSE.
I pray you, sir, receive the money now,
For fear you ne'er see chain nor money more.
ANGELO. You are a merry man, sir; fare you well.
Exit
ANTIPHOLUS OF SYRACUSE.
What I should think of this cannot tell:
But this I think, there's no man is so vain
That would refuse so fair an offer'd chain.
I see a man here needs not live by shifts,
When in the streets he meets such golden gifts.
I'll to the mart, and there for Dromio stay;
If any ship put out, then straight away.
Exit

ACT IV. SCENE 1

A public place
*Enter Second Merchant, Angelo, and an
Officer*
SECOND MERCHANT.
You know since Pentecost the sum is due,
And since I have not much importun'd you;
Nor now I had not, but that I am bound
To Persia, and want guilders for my voyage.
Therefore make present satisfaction,
Or I'll attach you by this officer.
ANGELO.
Even just the sum that I do owe to you
Is growing to me by Antipholus;
And in the instant that I met with you
He had of me a chain; at five o'clock
I shall receive the money for the same.
Pleaseth you walk with me down to his
house,
I will discharge my bond, and thank you too.
*Enter Antipholus Of Ephesus, and Dromio Of
Ephesus, from the Courtezan's*
OFFICER.
That labour may you save; see where he
comes.

ANTIPHOLUS OF EPHESUS.
While I go to the goldsmith's house, go thou
And buy a rope's end; that will I bestow
Among my wife and her confederates,
For locking me out of my doors by day.
But, soft, I see the goldsmith. Get thee
gone;
Buy thou a rope, and bring it home to me.
DROMIO OF EPHESUS.
I buy a thousand pound a year; I buy a rope.
Exit Dromio
ANTIPHOLUS OF EPHESUS.
A man is well holp up that trusts to you!
I promised your presence and the chain;
But neither chain nor goldsmith came to me.
Belike you thought our love would last too
long,
If it were chain'd together, and therefore
came not.
ANGELO.
Saving your merry humour, here's the note
How much your chain weighs to the utmost
carat,
The fineness of the gold, and chargeful
fashion,
Which doth amount to three odd ducats

more
Than I stand debted to this gentleman.
I pray you see him presently discharg'd,
For he is bound to sea, and stays but for it.

ANTIPHOLUS OF EPHESUS.
I am not furnish'd with the present money;
Besides, I have some business in the town.
Good signior, take the stranger to my house,
And with you take the chain, and bid my
wife
Disburse the sum on the receipt thereof.
Perchance I will be there as soon as you.

ANGELO.
Then you will bring the chain to her
yourself?

ANTIPHOLUS OF EPHESUS.
No; bear it with you, lest I come not time
enough.

ANGELO.
Well, sir, I will. Have you the chain about
you?

ANTIPHOLUS OF EPHESUS.
An if I have not, sir, I hope you have;
Or else you may return without your money.

ANGELO.
Nay, come, I pray you, sir, give me the

chain;
Both wind and tide stays for this gentleman,
And I, to blame, have held him here too
long.

ANTIPHOLUS OF EPHESUS.

Good Lord! you use this dalliance to excuse
Your breach of promise to the Porpentine;
I should have chid you for not bringing it,
But, like a shrew, you first begin to brawl.

SECOND MERCHANT.

The hour steals on; I pray you, sir, dispatch.

ANGELO.

You hear how he importunes methe chain!

ANTIPHOLUS OF EPHESUS.

Why, give it to my wife, and fetch your
money.

ANGELO.

Come, come, you know I gave it you even
now.
Either send the chain or send by me some
token.

ANTIPHOLUS OF EPHESUS.

Fie, now you run this humour out of breath!
Come, where's the chain? I pray you let me
see it.

SECOND MERCHANT.
My business cannot brook this dalliance.
Good sir, say whe'r you'll answer me or no;
If not, I'll leave him to the officer.
ANTIPHOLUS OF EPHESUS.
I answer you! What should I answer you?
ANGELO.
The money that you owe me for the chain.
ANTIPHOLUS OF EPHESUS.
I owe you none till I receive the chain.
ANGELO.
You know I gave it you half an hour since.
ANTIPHOLUS OF EPHESUS.
You gave me none; you wrong me much to
say so.
ANGELO.
You wrong me more, sir, in denying it.
Consider how it stands upon my credit.
SECOND MERCHANT.
Well, officer, arrest him at my suit.
OFFICER.
I do; and charge you in the Duke's name to
obey me.
ANGELO.
This touches me in reputation.
Either consent to pay this sum for me,

Or I attach you by this officer.
ANTIPHOLUS OF EPHESUS.
Consent to pay thee that I never had!
Arrest me, foolish fellow, if thou dar'st.
ANGELO.
Here is thy fee; arrest him, officer.
I would not spare my brother in this case,
If he should scorn me so apparently.
OFFICER.
I do arrest you, sir; you hear the suit.
ANTIPHOLUS OF EPHESUS.
I do obey thee till I give thee bail.
But, sirrah, you shall buy this sport as dear
As all the metal in your shop will answer.
ANGELO.
Sir, sir, I shall have law in Ephesus,
To your notorious shame, I doubt it not.
Enter Dromio Of Syracuse, from the bay
DROMIO OF SYRACUSE.
Master, there's a bark of Epidamnum
That stays but till her owner comes aboard,
And then, sir, she bears away. Our
fraughtage, sir,
I have convey'd aboard; and I have bought
The oil, the balsamum, and aquavitx.
The ship is in her trim; the merry wind

Blows fair from land; they stay for nought at an

But for their owner, master, and yourself.

ANTIPHOLUS OF EPHESUS.

How now! a madman? Why, thou peevish sheep,

What ship of Epidamnum stays for me?

DROMIO OF SYRACUSE.

A ship you sent me to, to hire waftage.

ANTIPHOLUS OF EPHESUS.

THOU drunken slave! I sent the for a rope;

And told thee to what purpose and what end.

DROMIO OF SYRACUSE.

YOU sent me for a rope's end as soon

You sent me to the bay, sir, for a bark.

ANTIPHOLUS OF EPHESUS.

I Will debate this matter at more leisure,

And teach your ears to list me with more heed.

To Adriana, villain, hie thee straight;

Give her this key, and tell her in the desk

That's cover'd o'er with Turkish tapestry

There is a purse of ducats; let her send it.

Tell her I am arrested in the street,

And that shall bail me; hie thee, slave, be

gone.
On, officer, to prison till it come.
Exeunt all but Dromio
DROMIO OF SYRACUSE.
To Adriana! that is where we din'd,
Where Dowsabel did claim me for her
husband.
She is too big, I hope, for me to compass.
Thither I must, although against my will,
For servants must their masters' minds
fulfil.
Exit

SCENE 2

The house of Antipholus Of Ephesus
Enter Adriana and Luciana

ADRIANA.
Ah, Luciana, did he tempt thee so?
Might'st thou perceive austerely in his eye
That he did plead in earnest? Yea or no?
Look'd he or red or pale, or sad or merrily?
What observation mad'st thou in this case
Of his heart's meteors tilting in his face?

LUCIANA.
First he denied you had in him no right.

ADRIANA.
He meant he did me nonethe more my spite.

LUCIANA.
Then swore he that he was a stranger here.

ADRIANA.
And true he swore, though yet forsworn he
were.

LUCIANA.
Then pleaded I for you.

ADRIANA.
And what said he?

LUCIANA.
That love I begg'd for you he begg'd of me.

73

ADRIANA.
With what persuasion did he tempt thy love?
LUCIANA.
With words that in an honest suit might move.
First he did praise my beauty, then my speech.
ADRIANA.
Didst speak him fair?
LUCIANA.
Have patience, I beseech.
ADRIANA.
I cannot, nor I will not hold me still;
My tongue, though not my heart, shall have his will.
He is deformed, crooked, old, and sere,
Illfac'd, worse bodied, shapeless everywhere;
Vicious, ungentle, foolish, blunt, unkind;
Stigmatical in making, worse in mind.
LUCIANA.
Who would be jealous then of such a one?
No evil lost is wail'd when it is gone.
ADRIANA.
Ah, but I think him better than I say,

And yet would herein others' eyes were
worse.
Far from her nest the lapwing cries away;
My heart prays for him, though my tongue
do curse.

Enter Dromio Of Syracuse.

DROMIO OF SYRACUSE.
Here gothe desk, the purse. Sweet now,
make haste.

LUCIANA.
How hast thou lost thy breath?

DROMIO OF SYRACUSE.
By running fast.

ADRIANA.
Where is thy master, Dromio? Is he well?

DROMIO OF SYRACUSE.
No, he's in Tartar limbo, worse than hell.
A devil in an everlasting garment hath him;
One whose hard heart is button'd up with
steel;
A fiend, a fairy, pitiless and rough;
A wolf, nay worse, a fellow all in buff;
A backfriend, a shoulderclapper, one that
countermands
The passages of alleys, creeks, and narrow
lands;

A hound that runs counter, and yet draws dryfoot well;
One that, before the Judgment, carries poor souls to hell.

ADRIANA.
Why, man, what is the matter?

DROMIO OF SYRACUSE.
I do not know the matter; he is rested on the case.

ADRIANA.
What, is he arrested? Tell me, at whose suit?

DROMIO OF SYRACUSE.
I know not at whose suit he is arrested well;
But he's in a suit of buff which 'rested him, that can I tell.
Will you send him, mistress, redemption, the money in his desk?

ADRIANA.
Go fetch it, sister.
[Exit Luciana]
This I wonder at:
Thus he unknown to me should be in debt.
Tell me, was he arrested on a band?

DROMIO OF SYRACUSE.
On a band, but on a stronger thing,

A chain, a chain. Do you not hear it ring?

ADRIANA.

What, the chain?

DROMIO OF SYRACUSE.

No, no, the bell; 'tis time that I were gone.
It was two ere I left him, and now the clock
strikes one.

ADRIANA.

The hours come back! That did I never hear.

DROMIO OF SYRACUSE.

O yes. If any hour meet a sergeant, 'a turns
back for very fear.

ADRIANA.

As if Time were in debt! How fondly dost
thou reason!

DROMIO OF SYRACUSE.

Time is a very bankrupt, and owes more
than he's worth to season.
Nay, he's a thief too: have you not heard
men say
That Time comes stealing on by night and
day?
If 'a be in debt and theft, and a sergeant in
the way,
Hath he not reason to turn back an hour in a
day?

Re-enter Luciana with a purse
ADRIANA.
Go, Dromio, there's the money; bear it straight,
And bring thy master home immediately.
Come, sister; I am press'd down with conceit
Conceit, my comfort and my injury.
Exeunt

SCENE 3

The mart
Enter Antipholus Of Syracuse
ANTIPHOLUS OF SYRACUSE.
There's not a man I meet but doth salute me
As if I were their wellacquainted friend;
And every one doth call me by my name.
Some tender money to me, some invite me,
Some other give me thanks for kindnesses,
Some offer me commodities to buy;
Even now a tailor call'd me in his shop,
And show'd me silks that he had bought for
me,
And therewithal took measure of my body.
Sure, these are but imaginary wiles,
And Lapland sorcerers inhabit here.
Enter Dromio Of Syracuse
DROMIO OF SYRACUSE.
Master, here's the gold you sent me for.
What, have you got the picture of old Adam
newapparell'd?
ANTIPHOLUS OF SYRACUSE.
What gold is this? What Adam dost thou
mean?

DROMIO OF SYRACUSE.
Not that Adam that kept the Paradise, but that Adam that keeps the prison; he that goes in the calf's skin that was kill'd for the Prodigal; he that came behind you, sir, like an evil angel, and bid you forsake your liberty.
ANTIPHOLUS OF SYRACUSE.
I understand thee not.
DROMIO OF SYRACUSE.
No? Why, 'tis a plain case: he that went, like a bassviol, in a case of leather; the man, sir, that, when gentlemen are tired, gives them a sob, and rest them; he, sir, that takes pity on decayed men, and give them suits of durance; he that sets up his rest to do more exploits with his mace than a morrispike.
ANTIPHOLUS OF SYRACUSE.
What, thou mean'st an officer?
DROMIO OF SYRACUSE.
Ay, sir, the sergeant of the band; that brings any man to answer it that breaks his band; on that thinks a man always going to bed, and says 'God give you good rest!'
ANTIPHOLUS OF SYRACUSE.
Well, sir, there rest in your foolery. Is there

any ship puts forth tonight? May we be gone?

DROMIO OF SYRACUSE.

Why, sir, I brought you word an hour since that the bark Expedition put forth tonight; and then were you hind'red by the sergeant, to tarry for the boy Delay. Here are the angels that you sent for to deliver you.

ANTIPHOLUS OF SYRACUSE.

The fellow is distract, and so am I;
And here we wander in illusions.
Some blessed power deliver us from hence!

Enter a Courtezan

COURTEZAN.

Well met, well met, Master Antipholus.
I see, sir, you have found the goldsmith now.
Is that the chain you promis'd me today?

ANTIPHOLUS OF SYRACUSE.

Satan, avoid! I charge thee, tempt me not.

DROMIO OF SYRACUSE.

Master, is this Mistress Satan?

ANTIPHOLUS OF SYRACUSE.

It is the devil.

DROMIO OF SYRACUSE.

Nay, she is worse, she is the devil's dam,

and here she comes in the habit of a light wench; and thereof comes that the wenches say 'God damn me!' That's as much to say 'God make me a light wench!' It is written they appear to men like angels of light; light is an effect of fire, and fire will burn; ergo, light wenches will burn. Come not near her.

COURTEZAN.

Your man and you are marvellous merry, sir. Will you go with me? We'll mend our dinner here.

DROMIO OF SYRACUSE.

Master, if you do, expect spoonmeat, or bespeak a long spoon.

ANTIPHOLUS OF SYRACUSE.

Why, Dromio?

DROMIO OF SYRACUSE.

Marry, he must have a long spoon that must eat with the devil.

ANTIPHOLUS OF SYRACUSE.

Avoid then, fiend! What tell'st thou me of supping?
Thou art, as you are all, a sorceress;
I conjure thee to leave me and be gone.

COURTEZAN.
Give me the ring of mine you had at dinner,
Or, for my diamond, the chain you promis'd,
And I'll be gone, sir, and not trouble you.
DROMIO OF SYRACUSE.
Some devils ask but the parings of one's
nail,
A rush, a hair, a drop of blood, a pin,
A nut, a cherrystone;
But she, more covetous, would have a chain.
Master, be wise; an if you give it her,
The devil will shake her chain, and fright us
with it.
COURTEZAN.
I pray you, sir, my ring, or else the chain;
I hope you do not mean to cheat me so.
ANTIPHOLUS OF SYRACUSE.
Avaunt, thou witch! Come, Dromio, let us
go.
DROMIO OF SYRACUSE.
'Fly pride' says the peacock. Mistress, that
you know.
*Exeunt Antipholus Of Syracuse and Dromio
Of Syracuse*
COURTEZAN.
Now, out of doubt, Antipholus is mad,

Else would he never so demean himself.
A ring he hath of mine worth forty ducats,
And for the same he promis'd me a chain;
Both one and other he denies me now.
The reason that I gather he is mad,
Besides this present instance of his rage,
Is a mad tale he told today at dinner
Of his own doors being shut against his
entrance.
Belike his wife, acquainted with his fits,
On purpose shut the doors against his way.
My way is now to hie home to his house,
And tell his wife that, being lunatic,
He rush'd into my house and took perforce
My ring away. This course I fittest choose,
For forty ducats is too much to lose.
Exit

SCENE 4

A street
Enter Antipholus Of Ephesus with the Officer

ANTIPHOLUS OF EPHESUS.
Fear me not, man; I will not break away.
I'll give thee, ere I leave thee, so much money,
To warrant thee, as I am 'rested for.
My wife is in a wayward mood today,
And will not lightly trust the messenger.
That I should be attach'd in Ephesus,
I tell you 'twill sound harshly in her cars.
Enter Dromio Of Ephesus, with a rope'send
Here comes my man; I think he brings the money.
How now, sir! Have you that I sent you for?
DROMIO OF EPHESUS.
Here's that, I warrant you, will pay them all.
ANTIPHOLUS OF EPHESUS.
But where's the money?
DROMIO OF EPHESUS.
Why, sir, I gave the money for the rope.
ANTIPHOLUS OF EPHESUS.
Five hundred ducats, villain, for rope?

DROMIO OF EPHESUS.
I'll serve you, sir, five hundred at the rate.
ANTIPHOLUS OF EPHESUS.
To what end did I bid thee hie thee home?
DROMIO OF EPHESUS.
To a rope'send, sir; and to that end am I
return'd.
ANTIPHOLUS OF EPHESUS.
And to that end, sir, I will welcome you.
[Beating him]
OFFICER.
Good sir, be patient.
DROMIO OF EPHESUS.
Nay, 'tis for me to be patient; I am in
adversity.
OFFICER.
Good now, hold thy tongue.
DROMIO OF EPHESUS.
Nay, rather persuade him to hold his hands.
ANTIPHOLUS OF EPHESUS.
Thou whoreson, senseless villain!
DROMIO OF EPHESUS.
I would I were senseless, sir, that I might
not feel your blows.
ANTIPHOLUS OF EPHESUS.
Thou art sensible in nothing but blows, and

so is an ass.

DROMIO OF EPHESUS.

I am an ass indeed; you may prove it by my long 'ears. I have served him from the hour of my nativity to this instant, and have nothing at his hands for my service but blows. When I am cold he heats me with beating; when I am warm he cools me with beating. I am wak'd with it when I sleep; rais'd with it when I sit; driven out of doors with it when I go from home; welcom'd home with it when I return; nay, I bear it on my shoulders as beggar wont her brat; and I think, when he hath lam'd me, I shall beg with it from door to door.

Enter Adriana, Luciana, The Courtezan, and a Schoolmaster call'd Pinch

ANTIPHOLUS OF EPHESUS.

Come, go along; my wife is coming yonder.

DROMIO OF EPHESUS.

Mistress, 'respice finem,' respect your end; or rather, to prophesy like the parrot, 'Beware the rope'send.'

ANTIPHOLUS OF EPHESUS.

Wilt thou still talk?

[Beating him]

COURTEZAN.
How say you now? Is not your husband
mad?
ADRIANA.
His incivility confirms no less.
Good Doctor Pinch, you are a conjurer:
Establish him in his true sense again,
And I will please you what you will demand.
LUCIANA.
Alas, how fiery and how sharp he looks!
COURTEZAN.
Mark how he trembles in his ecstasy.
PINCH.
Give me your hand, and let me feel your
pulse.
ANTIPHOLUS OF EPHESUS.
There is my hand, and let it feel your ear.
[Striking him]
PINCH.
I charge thee, Satan, hous'd within this
man,
To yield possession to my holy prayers,
And to thy state of darkness hie thee
straight.
I conjure thee by all the saints in heaven.

ANTIPHOLUS OF EPHESUS.
Peace, doting wizard, peace! I am not mad.
ADRIANA.
O, that thou wert not, poor distressed soul!
ANTIPHOLUS OF EPHESUS.
You minion, you, are these your customers?
Did this companion with the saffron face
Revel and feast it at my house today,
Whilst upon me the guilty doors were shut,
And I denied to enter in my house?
ADRIANA.
O husband, God doth know you din'd at
home,
Where would you had remain'd until this
time,
Free from these slanders and this open
shame!
ANTIPHOLUS OF EPHESUS.
Din'd at home! Thou villain, what sayest
thou?
DROMIO OF EPHESUS.
Sir, Sooth to say, you did not dine at home.
ANTIPHOLUS OF EPHESUS.
Were not my doors lock'd up and I shut out?
DROMIO OF EPHESUS.
Perdie, your doors were lock'd and you shut

out.

ANTIPHOLUS OF EPHESUS.

And did not she herself revile me there?

DROMIO OF EPHESUS.

Sans fable, she herself revil'd you there.

ANTIPHOLUS OF EPHESUS.

Did not her kitchenmaid rail, taunt, and scorn me?

DROMIO OF EPHESUS.

Certes, she did; the kitchenvestal scorn'd you.

ANTIPHOLUS OF EPHESUS.

And did not I in rage depart from thence?

DROMIO OF EPHESUS.

In verity, you did. My bones bear witness,
That since have felt the vigour of his rage.

ADRIANA.

Is't good to soothe him in these contraries?

PINCH.

It is no shame; the fellow finds his vein,
And, yielding to him, humours well his frenzy.

ANTIPHOLUS OF EPHESUS.

Thou hast suborn'd the goldsmith to arrest me.

ADRIANA.

Alas, I sent you money to redeem you,
By Dromio here, who came in haste for it.

DROMIO OF EPHESUS.

Money by me! Heart and goodwill you
might,
But surely, master, not a rag of money.

ANTIPHOLUS OF EPHESUS.

Went'st not thou to her for purse of ducats?

ADRIANA.

He came to me, and I deliver'd it.

LUCIANA.

And I am witness with her that she did.

DROMIO OF EPHESUS.

God and the ropemaker bear me witness
That I was sent for nothing but a rope!

PINCH. Mistress, both man and master is
possess'd;
I know it by their pale and deadly looks.
They must be bound, and laid in some dark
room.

ANTIPHOLUS OF EPHESUS.

Say, wherefore didst thou lock me forth
today?
And why dost thou deny the bag of gold?

ADRIANA.
I did not, gentle husband, lock thee forth.
DROMIO OF EPHESUS.
And, gentle master, I receiv'd no gold;
But I confess, sir, that we were lock'd out.
ADRIANA.
Dissembling villain, thou speak'st false in both.
ANTIPHOLUS OF EPHESUS.
Dissembling harlot, thou art false in all,
And art confederate with a damned pack
To make a loathsome abject scorn of me;
But with these nails I'll pluck out these false eyes
That would behold in me this shameful sport.
ADRIANA.
O, bind him, bind him; let him not come near me.
PINCH.
More company! The fiend is strong within him.
Enter three or four, and offer to bind him. He strives
LUCIANA.
Ay me, poor man, how pale and wan he

looks!

ANTIPHOLUS OF EPHESUS.
What, will you murder me? Thou gaoler,
thou,
I am thy prisoner. Wilt thou suffer them
To make a rescue?

OFFICER.
Masters, let him go;
He is my prisoner, and you shall not have
him.

PINCH.
Go bind this man, for he is frantic too.
[They bind DROMIO]

ADRIANA.
What wilt thou do, thou peevish officer?
Hast thou delight to see a wretched man
Do outrage and displeasure to himself?

OFFICER.
He is my prisoner; if I let him go,
The debt he owes will be requir'd of me.

ADRIANA.
I will discharge thee ere I go from thee;
Bear me forthwith unto his creditor,
And, knowing how the debt grows, I will pay
it.
Good Master Doctor, see him safe convey'd

Home to my house. O most unhappy day!
ANTIPHOLUS OF EPHESUS.
O most unhappy strumpet!
DROMIO OF EPHESUS.
Master, I am here ent'red in bond for you.
ANTIPHOLUS OF EPHESUS.
Out on thee, villian! Wherefore dost thou
mad me?
DROMIO OF EPHESUS.
Will you be bound for nothing?
Be mad, good master; cry 'The devil!'
LUCIANA.
God help, poor souls, how idly do they talk!
ADRIANA.
Go bear him hence. Sister, go you with me.
*Exeunt all but Adriana, Luciana, Officers,
and Courtezan Say now, whose suit is he
arrested at?*
OFFICER.
One Angelo, a goldsmith; do you know him?
ADRIANA.
I know the man. What is the sum he owes?
OFFICER.
Two hundred ducats.
ADRIANA.
Say, how grows it due?

OFFICER.
Due for a chain your husband had of him.
ADRIANA.
He did bespeak a chain for me, but had it
not.
COURTEZAN.
When as your husband, all in rage, today
Came to my house, and took away my ring
The ring I saw upon his finger now
Straight after did I meet him with a chain.
ADRIANA.
It may be so, but I did never see it.
Come, gaoler, bring me where the goldsmith
is;
I long to know the truth hereof at large.
*Enter Antipholus Of Syracuse, with his
rapier drawn, and Dromio Of Syracuse.*
LUCIANA.
God, for thy mercy! they are loose again.
ADRIANA.
And come with naked swords.
Let's call more help to have them bound
again.
OFFICER.
Away, they'll kill us!
Exeunt all but Antipholus Of Syracuse and

Dromio Of Syracuse as fast as may be, frighted

ANTIPHOLUS OF SYRACUSE.

I see these witches are afraid of swords.

DROMIO OF SYRACUSE.

She that would be your wife now ran from you.

ANTIPHOLUS OF SYRACUSE.

Come to the Centaur; fetch our stuff from thence.

I long that we were safe and sound aboard.

DROMIO OF SYRACUSE.

Faith, stay here this night; they will surely do us no harm; you saw they speak us fair, give us gold; methinks they are such a gentle nation that, but for the mountain of mad flesh that claims marriage of me, could find in my heart to stay here still and turn witch.

ANTIPHOLUS OF SYRACUSE.

I will not stay tonight for all the town; Therefore away, to get our stuff aboard.

Exeunt

ACT V. SCENE 1

A street before a priory
Enter Second Merchant and Angelo
ANGELO.
I am sorry, sir, that I have hind'red you;
But I protest he had the chain of me,
Though most dishonestly he doth deny it.
SECOND MERCHANT.
How is the man esteem'd here in the city?
ANGELO.
Of very reverend reputation, sir,
Of credit infinite, highly belov'd,
Second to none that lives here in the city;
His word might bear my wealth at any time.
SECOND MERCHANT.
Speak softly; yonder, as I think, he walks.
Enter Antipholus Of Syracuse and Dromio Of Syracuse
ANGELO.
'Tis so; and that self chain about his neck
Which he forswore most monstrously to have.
Good sir, draw near to me, I'll speak to him.
Signior Andpholus, I wonder much
That you would put me to this shame and

trouble;
And, not without some scandal to yourself,
With circumstance and oaths so to deny
This chain, which now you wear so openly.
Beside the charge, the shame,
imprisonment,
You have done wrong to this my honest
friend;
Who, but for staying on our controversy,
Had hoisted sail and put to sea today.
This chain you had of me; can you deny it?
ANTIPHOLUS OF SYRACUSE.
I think I had; I never did deny it.
SECOND MERCHANT.
Yes, that you did, sir, and forswore it too.
ANTIPHOLUS OF SYRACUSE.
Who heard me to deny it or forswear it?
SECOND MERCHANT.
These ears of mine, thou know'st, did hear
thee.
Fie on thee, wretch! 'tis pity that thou liv'st
To walk where any honest men resort.
ANTIPHOLUS OF SYRACUSE.
Thou art a villain to impeach me thus;
I'll prove mine honour and mine honesty
Against thee presently, if thou dar'st stand.

SECOND MERCHANT.
I dare, and do defy thee for a villain.
[They draw]
Enter Adriana, Luciana, the Courtezan, and Others
ADRIANA.
Hold, hurt him not, for God's sake! He is mad.
Some get within him, take his sword away;
Bind Dromio too, and bear them to my house.
DROMIO OF SYRACUSE.
Run, master, run; for God's sake take a house.
This is some priory. In, or we are spoil'd.
Exeunt Antipholus Of Syracuse and Dromio Of Syracuse to the priory
Enter the Lady Abbess
ABBESS.
Be quiet, people. Wherefore throng you hither?
ADRIANA.
To fetch my poor distracted husband hence.
Let us come in, that we may bind him fast,
And bear him home for his recovery.

ANGELO.
I knew he was not in his perfect wits.
SECOND MERCHANT.
I am sorry now that I did draw on him.
ABBESS.
How long hath this possession held the
man?
ADRIANA.
This week he hath been heavy, sour, sad,
And much different from the man he was;
But till this afternoon his passion
Ne'er brake into extremity of rage.
ABBESS.
Hath he not lost much wealth by wreck of
sea?
Buried some dear friend? Hath not else his
eye
Stray'd his affection in unlawful love?
A sin prevailing much in youthful men
Who give their eyes the liberty of gazing.
Which of these sorrows is he subject to?
ADRIANA.
To none of these, except it be the last;
Namely, some love that drew him oft from
home.

ABBESS.
You should for that have reprehended him.
ADRIANA.
Why, so I did.
ABBESS.
Ay, but not rough enough.
ADRIANA.
As roughly as my modesty would let me.
ABBESS.
Haply in private.
ADRIANA.
And in assemblies too.
ABBESS.
Ay, but not enough.
ADRIANA.
It was the copy of our conference.
In bed, he slept not for my urging it;
At board, he fed not for my urging it;
Alone, it was the subject of my theme;
In company, I often glanced it;
Still did I tell him it was vile and bad.
ABBESS.
And thereof came it that the man was mad.
The venom clamours of a jealous woman
Poisons more deadly than a mad dog's
tooth.

It seems his sleeps were hind'red by thy railing,
And thereof comes it that his head is light.
Thou say'st his meat was sauc'd with thy upbraidings:
Unquiet meals make ill digestions;
Thereof the raging fire of fever bred;
And what's a fever but a fit of madness?
Thou say'st his sports were hind'red by thy brawls.
Sweet recreation barr'd, what doth ensue
But moody and dull melancholy,
Kinsman to grim and comfortless despair,
And at her heels a huge infectious troop
Of pale distemperatures and foes to life?
In food, in sport, and lifepreserving rest,
To be disturb'd would mad or man or beast.
The consequence is, then, thy jealous fits
Hath scar'd thy husband from the use of wits.

LUCIANA.
She never reprehended him but mildly,
When he demean'd himself rough, rude, and wildly.
Why bear you these rebukes, and answer not?

ADRIANA.
She did betray me to my own reproof.
Good people, enter, and lay hold on him.
ABBESS.
No, not a creature enters in my house.
ADRIANA.
Then let your servants bring my husband
forth.
ABBESS.
Neither; he took this place for sanctuary,
And it shall privilege him from your hands
Till I have brought him to his wits again,
Or lose my labour in assaying it.
ADRIANA.
I will attend my husband, be his nurse,
Diet his sickness, for it is my office,
And will have no attorney but myself;
And therefore let me have him home with
me.
ABBESS.
Be patient; for I will not let him stir
Till I have us'd the approved means I have,
With wholesome syrups, drugs, and holy
prayers,
To make of him a formal man again.
It is a branch and parcel of mine oath,

A charitable duty of my order;
Therefore depart, and leave him here with
me.

ADRIANA.

I will not hence and leave my husband here;
And ill it doth beseem your holiness
To separate the husband and the wife.

ABBESS.

Be quiet, and depart; thou shalt not have
him.

Exit

LUCIANA.

Complain unto the Duke of this indignity.

ADRIANA.

Come, go; I will fall prostrate at his feet,
And never rise until my tears and prayers
Have won his Grace to come in person hither
And take perforce my husband from the
Abbess.

SECOND MERCHANT.

By this, I think, the dial points at five;
Anon, I'm sure, the Duke himself in person
Comes this way to the melancholy vale,
The place of death and sorry execution,
Behind the ditches of the abbey here.

ANGELO.
Upon what cause?
SECOND MERCHANT.
To see a reverend Syracusian merchant,
Who put unluckily into this bay
Against the laws and statutes of this town,
Beheaded publicly for his offence.
ANGELO.
See where they come; we will behold his
death.
LUCIANA.
Kneel to the Duke before he pass the abbey.
*Enter the Duke, attended; Aegeon,
bareheaded; with the Headsman and other
Officers*
DUKE.
Yet once again proclaim it publicly,
If any friend will pay the sum for him,
He shall not die; so much we tender him.
ADRIANA.
Justice, most sacred Duke, against the
Abbess!
DUKE.
She is a virtuous and a reverend lady;
It cannot be that she hath done thee wrong.

ADRIANA.
May it please your Grace, Antipholus, my husband,
Who I made lord of me and all I had
At your important lettersthis ill day
A most outrageous fit of madness took him,
That desp'rately he hurried through the street,
With him his bondman all as mad as he,
Doing displeasure to the citizens
By rushing in their houses, bearing thence
Rings, jewels, anything his rage did like.
Once did I get him bound and sent him home,
Whilst to take order for the wrongs I went,
That here and there his fury had committed.
Anon, I wot not by what strong escape,
He broke from those that had the guard of him,
And with his mad attendant and himself,
Each one with ireful passion, with drawn swords,
Met us again and, madly bent on us,
Chas'd us away; till, raising of more aid,
We came again to bind them. Then they fled
Into this abbey, whither we pursu'd them;

And here the Abbess shuts the gates on us,
And will not suffer us to fetch him out,
Nor send him forth that we may bear him hence.
Therefore, most gracious Duke, with thy command
Let him be brought forth and borne hence for help.

DUKE.
Long since thy husband serv'd me in my wars,
And I to thee engag'd a prince's word,
When thou didst make him master of thy bed,
To do him all the grace and good I could.
Go, some of you, knock at the abbey gate,
And bid the Lady Abbess come to me,
I will determine this before I stir.

Enter a Messenger

MESSENGER.
O mistress, mistress, shift and save yourself!
My master and his man are both broke loose,
Beaten the maids arow and bound the doctor,

Whose beard they have sing'd off with brands of fire;
And ever, as it blaz'd, they threw on him
Great pails of puddled mire to quench the hair.
My master preaches patience to him, and the while
His man with scissors nicks him like a fool;
And sure, unless you send some present help,
Between them they will kill the conjurer.
ADRIANA.
Peace, fool! thy master and his man are here,
And that is false thou dost report to us.
MESSENGER.
Mistress, upon my life, I tell you true;
I have not breath'd almost since I did see it.
He cries for you, and vows, if he can take you,
To scorch your face, and to disfigure you.
[Cry within]
Hark, hark, I hear him, mistress; fly, be gone!
DUKE.
Come, stand by me; fear nothing. Guard with

halberds.

ADRIANA.

Ay me, it is my husband! Witness you
That he is borne about invisible.
Even now we hous'd him in the abbey here,
And now he's there, past thought of human
reason.

*Enter Antipholus Ofephesus and Dromio
Ofephesus*

ANTIPHOLUS OFEPHESUS.

Justice, most gracious Duke; O, grant me
justice!
Even for the service that long since I did
thee,
When I bestrid thee in the wars, and took
Deep scars to save thy life; even for the
blood
That then I lost for thee, now grant me
justice.

AEGEON.

Unless the fear of death doth make me
dote,
I see my son Antipholus, and Dromio.

ANTIPHOLUS OFEPHESUS.

Justice, sweet Prince, against that woman
there!

She whom thou gav'st to me to be my wife,
That hath abused and dishonoured me
Even in the strength and height of injury.
Beyond imagination is the wrong
That she this day hath shameless thrown on me.

DUKE.
Discover how, and thou shalt find me just.

ANTIPHOLUS OFEPHESUS.
This day, great Duke, she shut the doors upon me,
While she with harlots feasted in my house.

DUKE.
A grievous fault. Say, woman, didst thou so?

ADRIANA.
No, my good lord. Myself, he, and my sister,
Today did dine together. So befall my soul
As this is false he burdens me withal!

LUCIANA.
Ne'er may I look on day nor sleep on night
But she tells to your Highness simple truth!

ANGELO.
O peflur'd woman! They are both forsworn.
In this the madman justly chargeth them.

ANTIPHOLUS OF EPHESUS.
My liege, I am advised what I say;

Neither disturbed with the effect of wine,
Nor headyrash, provok'd with raging ire,
Albeit my wrongs might make one wiser
mad.
This woman lock'd me out this day from
dinner;
That goldsmith there, were he not pack'd
with her,
Could witness it, for he was with me then;
Who parted with me to go fetch a chain,
Promising to bring it to the Porpentine,
Where Balthazar and I did dine together.
Our dinner done, and he not coming thither,
I went to seek him. In the street I met him,
And in his company that gentleman.
There did this perjur'd goldsmith swear me
down
That I this day of him receiv'd the chain,
Which, God he knows, I saw not; for the
which
He did arrest me with an officer.
I did obey, and sent my peasant home
For certain ducats; he with none return'd.
Then fairly I bespoke the officer
To go in person with me to my house.
By th' way we met my wife, her sister, and a

rabble more
Of vile confederates. Along with them
They brought one Pinch, a hungry leanfac'd
villain,
A mere anatomy, a mountebank,
A threadbare juggler, and a fortuneteller,
A needy, hollowey'd, sharplooking wretch,
A living dead man. This pernicious slave,
Forsooth, took on him as a conjurer,
And gazing in mine eyes, feeling my pulse,
And with no face, as 'twere, outfacing me,
Cries out I was possess'd. Then all together
They fell upon me, bound me, bore me
thence,
And in a dark and dankish vault at home
There left me and my man, both bound
together;
Till, gnawing with my teeth my bonds in
sunder,
I gain'd my freedom, and immediately
Ran hither to your Grace; whom I beseech
To give me ample satisfaction
For these deep shames and great
indignities.
ANGELO.
My lord, in truth, thus far I witness with

him,
That he din'd not at home, but was lock'd out.
DUKE.
But had he such a chain of thee, or no?
ANGELO.
He had, my lord, and when he ran in here,
These people saw the chain about his neck.
SECOND MERCHANT.
Besides, I will be sworn these ears of mine
Heard you confess you had the chain of him,
After you first forswore it on the mart;
And thereupon I drew my sword on you,
And then you fled into this abbey here,
From whence, I think, you are come by miracle.
ANTIPHOLUS OF EPHESUS.
I never came within these abbey walls,
Nor ever didst thou draw thy sword on me;
I never saw the chain, so help me Heaven!
And this is false you burden me withal.
DUKE.
Why, what an intricate impeach is this!
I think you all have drunk of Circe's cup.
If here you hous'd him, here he would have been;

If he were mad, he would not plead so
coldly.
You say he din'd at home: the goldsmith
here
Denies that saying. Sirrah, what say you?
DROMIO OF EPHESUS.
Sir, he din'd with her there, at the
Porpentine.
COURTEZAN.
He did; and from my finger snatch'd that
ring.
ANTIPHOLUS OF EPHESUS.
'Tis true, my liege; this ring I had of her.
DUKE.
Saw'st thou him enter at the abbey here?
COURTEZAN.
As sure, my liege, as I do see your Grace.
DUKE.
Why, this is strange. Go call the Abbess
hither.
I think you are all mated or stark mad.
Exit one to the Abbess
AEGEON.
Most mighty Duke, vouchsafe me speak a
word:
Haply I see a friend will save my life

And pay the sum that may deliver me.
DUKE.
Speak freely, Syracusian, what thou wilt.
AEGEON.
Is not your name, sir, call'd Antipholus?
And is not that your bondman Dromio?
DROMIO OF EPHESUS.
Within this hour I was his bondman, sir,
But he, I thank him, gnaw'd in two my cords
Now am I Dromio and his man unbound.
AEGEON.
I am sure you both of you remember me.
DROMIO OF EPHESUS.
Ourselves we do remember, sir, by you;
For lately we were bound as you are now.
You are not Pinch's patient, are you, sir?
AEGEON.
Why look you strange on me? You know me
well.
ANTIPHOLUS OF EPHESUS.
I never saw you in my life till now.
AEGEON.
O! grief hath chang'd me since you saw me
last;
And careful hours with time's deformed
hand

Have written strange defeatures in my face.
But tell me yet, dost thou not know my
voice?
ANTIPHOLUS OF EPHESUS.
Neither.
AEGEON.
Dromio, nor thou?
DROMIO OF EPHESUS.
No, trust me, sir, nor I.
AEGEON.
I am sure thou dost.
DROMIO OF EPHESUS.
Ay, sir, but I am sure I do not; and
whatsoever a man denies, you are now
bound to believe him.
AEGEON.
Not know my voice! O time's extremity,
Hast thou so crack'd and splitted my poor
tongue
In seven short years that here my only son
Knows not my feeble key of untun'd cares?
Though now this grained face of mine be hid
In sapconsuming winter's drizzled snow,
And all the conduits of my blood froze up,
Yet hath my night of life some memory,
My wasting lamps some fading glimmer

left,
My dull deaf ears a little use to hear;
All these old witnessesI cannot err
Tell me thou art my son Antipholus.
ANTIPHOLUS OF EPHESUS.
I never saw my father in my life.
AEGEON.
But seven years since, in Syracuse, boy,
Thou know'st we parted; but perhaps, my
son,
Thou sham'st to acknowledge me in misery.
ANTIPHOLUS OF EPHESUS.
The Duke and all that know me in the city
Can witness with me that it is not so:
I ne'er saw Syracuse in my life.
DUKE.
I tell thee, Syracusian, twenty years
Have I been patron to Antipholus,
During which time he ne'er saw Syracuse.
I see thy age and dangers make thee dote.
*Re-enter the Abbess, with Antipholus Of
Syracuse and Dromio Of Syracuse*
ABBESS.
Most mighty Duke, behold a man much
wrong'd.
[All gather to see them]

ADRIANA.
I see two husbands, or mine eyes deceive me.
DUKE.
One of these men is genius to the other;
And so of these. Which is the natural man,
And which the spirit? Who deciphers them?
DROMIO OF SYRACUSE.
I, sir, am Dromio; command him away.
DROMIO OF EPHESUS.
I, Sir, am Dromio; pray let me stay.
ANTIPHOLUS OF SYRACUSE.
Aegeon, art thou not? or else his
DROMIO OF SYRACUSE.
O, my old master! who hath bound
ABBESS.
Whoever bound him, I will loose his bonds,
And gain a husband by his liberty.
Speak, old Aegeon, if thou be'st the man
That hadst a wife once call'd Aemilia,
That bore thee at a burden two fair sons.
O, if thou be'st the same Aegeon, speak,
And speak unto the same Aemilia!
AEGEON.
If I dream not, thou art Aemilia.
If thou art she, tell me where is that son

That floated with thee on the fatal raft?

ABBESS.

By men of Epidamnum he and I
And the twin Dromio, all were taken up;
But by and by rude fishermen of Corinth
By force took Dromio and my son from
them,
And me they left with those of Epidamnum.
What then became of them I cannot tell;
I to this fortune that you see me in.

DUKE.

Why, here begins his morning story right.
These two Antipholus', these two so like,
And these two Dromios, one in semblance
Besides her urging of her wreck at sea
These are the parents to these children,
Which accidentally are met together.
Antipholus, thou cam'st from Corinth first?

ANTIPHOLUS OF SYRACUSE.

No, sir, not I; I came from Syracuse.

DUKE.

Stay, stand apart; I know not which is which.

ANTIPHOLUS OF EPHESUS.

I came from Corinth, my most gracious lord.

DROMIO OF EPHESUS.

And I with him.

ANTIPHOLUS OF EPHESUS.
Brought to this town by that most famous warrior,
Duke Menaphon, your most renowned uncle.
ADRIANA.
Which of you two did dine with me today?
ANTIPHOLUS OF SYRACUSE.
I, gentle mistress.
ADRIANA.
And are not you my husband?
ANTIPHOLUS OF EPHESUS.
No; I say nay to that.
ANTIPHOLUS OF SYRACUSE.
And so do I, yet did she call me so;
And this fair gentlewoman, her sister here,
Did call me brother. *[To Luciana]* What I told you then,
I hope I shall have leisure to make good;
If this be not a dream I see and hear.
ANGELO.
That is the chain, sir, which you had of me.
ANTIPHOLUS OF SYRACUSE.
I think it be, sir; I deny it not.
ANTIPHOLUS OF EPHESUS.
And you, sir, for this chain arrested me.

ANGELO.
I think I did, sir; I deny it not.
ADRIANA.
I sent you money, sir, to be your bail,
By Dromio; but I think he brought it not.
DROMIO OF EPHESUS.
No, none by me.
ANTIPHOLUS OF SYRACUSE.
This purse of ducats I receiv'd from you,
And Dromio my man did bring them me.
I see we still did meet each other's man,
And I was ta'en for him, and he for me,
And thereupon these ERRORS are arose.
ANTIPHOLUS OF EPHESUS.
These ducats pawn I for my father here.
DUKE.
It shall not need; thy father hath his life.
COURTEZAN.
Sir, I must have that diamond from you.
ANTIPHOLUS OF EPHESUS.
There, take it; and much thanks for my good
cheer.
ABBESS.
Renowned Duke, vouchsafe to take the
pains
To go with us into the abbey here,

And hear at large discoursed all our
fortunes;
And all that are assembled in this place
That by this sympathized one day's error
Have suffer'd wrong, go keep us company,
And we shall make full satisfaction.
Thirtythree years have I but gone in travail
Of you, my sons; and till this present hour
My heavy burden ne'er delivered.
The Duke, my husband, and my children
both,
And you the calendars of their nativity,
Go to a gossips' feast, and go with me;
After so long grief, such nativity!
DUKE.
With all my heart, I'll gossip at this feast.
*Exeunt all but Antipholus Of Syracuse,
Antipholus Of Ephesus, Dromio Of Syracuse,
and Dromio Of Ephesus*
DROMIO OF SYRACUSE.
Master, shall I fetch your stuff from
shipboard?
ANTIPHOLUS OF EPHESUS.
Dromio, what stuff of mine hast thou
embark'd?

DROMIO OF SYRACUSE.
Your goods that lay at host, sir, in the
Centaur.
ANTIPHOLUS OF SYRACUSE.
He speaks to me. I am your master, Dromio.
Come, go with us; we'll look to that anon.
Embrace thy brother there; rejoice with him.
Exeunt Antipholus Of Syracuse and
Antipholus Of Ephesus
DROMIO OF SYRACUSE.
There is a fat friend at your master's house,
That kitchen'd me for you today at dinner;
She now shall be my sister, not my wife.
DROMIO OF EPHESUS.
Methinks you are my glass, and not my
brother;
I see by you I am a sweetfac'd youth.
Will you walk in to see their gossiping?
DROMIO OF SYRACUSE.
Not I, sir; you are my elder.
DROMIO OF EPHESUS.
That's a question; how shall we try it?
DROMIO OF SYRACUSE.
We'll draw cuts for the senior; till then, lead
thou first.

DROMIO OF EPHESUS.
Nay, then, thus:
We came into the world like brother and
brother,
And now let's go hand in hand, not one
before another.
Exeunt

THE END

Printed in the United States
108228LV00004B/499/A